Partly Sane, Prose Merry and Rhyme

David Hogarth

Partly Sane, Prose Merry and Rhyme

Text copyright©2025 David Hogarth
Cover: Ribeiro

ISBN 978-1-7393239-9-8

The Author has asserted his rights under the Copyright, Designs and Patents Act 1988 to be identified as the author of this work.

Conditions of Sale
No part of this book may be reproduced or transmitted by any means without the permission of the publisher.

British Library Cataloguing in Publication Data.
A catalogue record for this book is available from the British Library.

1 3 5 4 2

First Published in Great Britain
Hawkwood Books 2025
Blackpool Enterprise Centre FY4 1EW

Printed and bound in Great Britain by CPI Group (UK) Ltd.
Croydon CR0 4YY

Partly Sane, Prose Merry and Rhyme

No Doubt - I

Alone I hear a whispered voice
That taunts and draws me out,
It tempts me to believe and dream
Then tortures me with doubt.
It guides my hand and feeds my mind
To lessen my mistakes,
Then walks away with smirking face
A broken man it makes.
It visits when I least expect
An uninvited guest,
Arriving just in time to spoil
A chance to be my best.
Who would invite this loser in
To mock and critique me?
And then I recognise the voice,
It's me, it's me, it's me.

There are good times and bad times, and you can be sure there will be more of both.

There is only one person you can always trust and never doubt... yourself.

Written verse is the word equivalent of music.

If poetry taps on your window in the middle of the night, be brave and let it in.

Thank you to all the poets who hear, see, feel, and think differently, in particular: Spike Milligan, Ian Dury, Pam Ayres.

Free Speech

Beware the arrogant elitists and their moralising ways,
Here to save us all, they say, from evil hateful days.
Blaming you for everything, even things you didn't do,
Trying to control your mind and change your point of view.
You're offensive, insensitive, vulgar and crude,
Unenlightened and stupid, totally rude.
A long way from home, where the righteous reside,
A blizzard of snowflakes with limitless pride.
They snigger and sneer full of boastful contempt,
A whole host of angels all twisted and bent.
So ready your soul for what comes next,
Good and evil written down between each line of text.
Hold on tight and don't let go, blank papers in the breeze,
There comes a growing perfect storm,
To wipe away the sleaze.

Big Issue?

Champagne, tinsel, and a packet of crisps,
What more could one need for a bash?
Just don't post it online,
Or in a short span of time,
You'll have thousands
Attempting to crash.

Supercilious

I've always been super silly, me,
But only me, not us.
You can make your own mind up,
So please don't make a fuss.
Don't keep banging on and on
And on and on and on,
How you think we all should be,
I care not a tinker's cuss.
Nor do I give a flying fart
Regarding your transparency,
For all I care, your 'savoir faire',
Is not worth tuppence to me.
But that's just me being silly, me,
Not you, them, they or us.
Just give your clucking mouth a rest,
You're supercilious.

Twenty Twenty-Two

New year comes but once a year,
It's three-six-five as usual.
Be who you are,
A shining star,
This really is quite crucial.

Young Guns

Write your stories now, you kids,
Write them thick and fast.
Write them with your heart and soul,
Lean back upon your past.
Write them in the here and now,
Write them up ahead,
Then when you've finished writing,
Clean your teeth and go to bed.

Enough is Enough

Of the things I require,
As opposed to desire,
I have plenty of all that I need.
If I had too much more,
I am almost quite sure,
That the total would equal pure greed.

Wood and Trees

There once was a man who was odd,
Who was happy to accept there was God,
But he failed how to see
That a tree could not be
When it stood there alone on its tod.

Reasons to be Silly - 1, 2, 3

Half a pound of silly,
Warm, and then it's chilly,
Tickle on a filly.
People in a hurry,
Always have to worry,
Go and get a curry.
Yards and yards apart,
Anxious off the chart,
Stop before you start.
Sit and take your time,
Coconut and lime,
Rock and roll in rhyme.
Everyone's a critic,
See an ad and click it,
Rather watch the cricket.
Baseless fears and lies,
Open your mince pies,
Spirits on the rise.
Give the dog a bone,
Always on your phone,
Need another loan.
Grab a bacon barm,
Surely do no harm,
Welcome to the farm.
Pie and mash and bitter,
Lovely laugh and titter,
Have a little twitter.
Better count to three,
There is no money tree,
Everything is free...
Reasons to be silly - 1, 2, 3.

To See or not To See

The more I see,
The more I think
Of boiling, toiling trouble.
I hope that time will prove me wrong
And burst this hubble bubble.

In at the Deep End

A lot depends on what we do,
Not what we say or think.
There is no doubt it's harder to
Swim on than stop and sink.

The Survey Show

Latest research now suggests
Something fishy is afoot,
Which can't be good for anyone,
No whats or ifs or buts.
But who is doing all the work?
We haven't got a clue.
That's right, it isn't anyone,
Including me and you.

AI spy with my little AI something beginning with aitch

Here to help in every way,
That simple humans can't.
A brand-new type of death machine
That lives up to its hype.
It adds up here,
It subtracts there,
A calculating hero.
And now to solve its greatest quiz,
How humans equal zero.

Abridged Too Far

That book really offends me,
It shouldn't be allowed to exist.
Well, you're here, and you're offensive,
So, pipe down and learn to resist.

Life's a Gas

The price of gas is going up,
It seems the sky's the limit.
It's being passed down, as usual,
To us what suffers... innit?

Up The Mighty Pool

'Yes, we have no bananas,'
Sang the man with the duck at halftime.
Then Sudds stuck one in the top corner
With the free kick he did time after time.
Hutchy zig-zagged down the touchline,
Then crossed for big Fred to head in,
Greenie would leave them all dizzy,
Setting up chance after chance for the win.
Micky Burns cuts inside past a couple,
Then plants a scorcher that no one could save,
Bob Hatton scores another three belters,
Sticking his head in where only the brave.
Budgie made keeping look easy,
Saving shot after shot every game,
Then Walshy nets goal of the season,
And bags his place in the Pool's Hall of Fame.
Too many more stars to be mentioned,
Have lit up Blackpool's own Bloomfield Road sky,
But they all live on bright in the memory,
And they will till the day that I die.
Sea... Sea... Seasiders!

The Party's Over

Turn out the lights,
The party's over.
Too many grey areas to examine.
Crack on with the real stuff,
Cause we've all heard enough.
Here comes pestilence, war, and famine.

The Long and the Short

Life is too short…
Say the people who know.
They have insider info on ages.
But how long is too long?
Ask the curious few.
Existence is a number of stages.

Go deh, Dready, Go deh

The sound of human noise
Is a thing that drives me batty.
I'd much rather listen to reggae -
Bang bop diddly go deh natty.

Good Old Maj

Put out your flags,
And eat some jelly,
Her Maj the Queen
Is on the telly!
She's done us good,
She's steered us straight,
Just where and why
Is pure debate.
The cheering crowds
With smiling faces
Are in no doubt
About their places.
They line the mall
And wait to see
Their good Queen Liz,
And all for free
Then off they trudge,
The weary crowd,
With not much bread -
But cake's allowed.

Reasons to be Silly - 4, 5, 6

Nicky nocky noodle,
Labrador and poodle,
Cream on apple strudel.
Milly Molly Mandy,
Rot your teeth with candy,
Wide awake and randy.
Piggy in the middle,
Always on the fiddle,
What a taradiddle!
Looking for a reason,
Changes in the season,
Just a hint of treason.
Eye upon the ball,
Something very small,
Back against the wall.
Look before you leap,
Check to see how deep,
Take a little peep.
More or less the same,
Portion out the blame,
All but those in name.
Try and find a fix,
Pick up all your sticks.
Reasons to be silly – 4, 5, 6.

Hey, Diddle-Fiddle

By the light of the silvery moon,
There's a cow and a dish
And a dog with a spoon.
Well, that's all diddle-diddle,
Said a cat with a fiddle,
Who proceeded to play a fine tune.

St. Georges Day, Apocalypse Siren Warning, Kick off 3 p.m.

St. George's Day,
A day to be proud,
To celebrate defeating the dragon.
Some will head out,
Some will stay in,
Especially all those with a tag on.
Have fun in the sun,
Your race isn't run.
When the siren of doom dials your phone,
Hey, do me a favour,
We aren't your slave labour,
Just fuck off and leave us alone.

Natural-istic

Nature will do as she chooses,
She won't ask permission from you.
She's been here quite a while as it happens,
And knows precisely just what she must do.

Times Past

At the end of the day,
When all's said and done,
And the bright lights have faded to blue.
There's a time and a place for everything,
Whether older or borrowed or new.

Eternal Spring

So much is best forgotten.
I've notten gotten lots of things,
But some things I do rely on
Are those hope eternal springs.

Super-Stupor

Everything is super.
Super-duper super-cool,
Super-this and super-that,
Super-silly super-fool,
Super-happy super-crappy,
Super-stupid super-smart,
Super-duper half-baked beings,
Super-stupor, apple-tart.
Super-horny super-scrawny,
Super-bad, super-sad,
Super-wealthy, super-healthy,
Super-stealthy, super-glad,
Super-savvy super-chavvy,
Super-shiny, super-glam,
Super-skilful, super-lingual,
Super-woman, super-man.

Rootin' Tootin' Shootin' Putin

To root the blinkin' Nazis out,
You have to start the lootin'.
Despite there being no toot to root,
Here's big guns, shootin' Putin.

The Creator

Creation isn't artificial,
It takes imagination and a whole lot more.
You think and you dream and you wish first,
Then you knock on that magical door.
Sometimes the door doesn't open,
They're busy preparing the stage.
Intelligence is a question of learning,
Playing your part is a coming of age.

High Wire

Where do your messages come from?
The ones that arrive in your mind?
From Fed-Ex, the web, or by E-mail?
Or is it playback, after search key and find?
Does it happen when you aren't even thinking?
Like a download from somewhere quite odd?
Or do we all have a line that's connected?
To a switchboard controller called God?

The Old Man and his Tea

I have to find out, what life is about,
Said the old man who sailed out to sea.
The oceans are deep,
Many secrets they keep,
Sorry, can't stop, I'm off out for tea.

Washington Redfaces

Megan Rapinoe missed her shot from the spot,
Her wretched attempt was a shocker.
The Swedes were not mashed,
But the US got trashed,
Guess the fans have good reason to mock her.

Standing in the Road

I've got my flag, and my placard too,
I'm off to a peaceful protest.
I promise to be good and not misbehave,
By just being a middle of the road pest.

Man... United

He's coming for you,
Make no mistake,
The horny red guy
With the spear.
So seek faith while you can,
And stand up, you're a man!
Then the path of escape will be clear.

I'm Not That Kind of Girl

To judge a trial it helps to know
The truth by definition.
But things are so confusing now,
With juxta disposition.
How on earth am I supposed
To see your real agenda
When all I have to go on
Is you're such a great pretender?

Guess What?

Again, I've written nought a poem,
And time is really pressing.
Is this a poem,
Or simply words?
I love to keep folks guessing.

Global Boiling

So now it's all 'global boiling'?
Third degree burns if you fall.
It's cooler if you're a bit smaller
Than for those who are physically tall.
Heat rises you see, so it's wiser
To lie low and enjoy a few beers.
They've looked in some books and decided
That it's hotter than all other years.

Danger to Life - Weather Update

I used to quite like Laura Tobin,
But now she just gets on me tits.
She claims that the world is on fire,
That our planet is falling to bits.
She must be right, she's on telly,
All her maps are bright orange and red,
Her forecasts are a 'Danger to Life' now,
She's quite certain we'll all soon be dead.

Reasons to Continue Being Silly - 7, 8, 9

Relatively speaking,
The roof is clearly leaking,
Needs a bit of tweaking.
Keep it hale and hearty,
Get a chance to party,
Don't dress up too tarty.
Open up and grow,
Start off way down low,
Steer into the know.
Wait and see what gives,
Then who dies and lives,
Life is such a swizz.
Jam and peanut brittle,
Large and then quite little,
Turn your tattle tittle.
Hands across the sea,
Nothing comes for free,
Sorrow into glee.
What is mine is mine,
Written verse and rhyme,
Try and find the time...
Reasons to be silly – 7, 8, 9.

All at Sea

Do no harm,
Laugh and cry,
Eat and drink,
Fail but try.
Wait and see
Go and get,
Open up,
Have we met?
Stand up tall,
Lay down low,
All at sea,
Row, row, row.

Stopwatch

Does anyone have the right time?
'There is no such thing,' said the clock.
Nobody knows when it started,
So, keep watching. You'll know when to stop.

One Story, Two Sides

Red or blue, red or blue,
Pick a colour, one or two.
Red or blue, red or blue,
Keep your mind a constant hue.

A Midsummer's Nice Scream

Here it comes, the longest day.
The sun will put his hat on,
A chance to mingle, breathe and hug
Instead of just being shat on.
The flavours that you have to choose
Are varied and so many.
Pick wisely as you make your choice,
Them those, these they, not any.
For choosing is a human thing,
It's nice to have a team.
Be sure to pick the one you like,
A midsummer's night dream.

Dead-End

Let's play doctors and nurses,
And undress to see what we can find.
Your list of ailments seems endless,
Every illness that's known to mankind.
I've given you a thorough check-up
And can find nothing to worry your head.
No problems or issues impending,
Take these tablets until you are dead.

Party Political Bored Fest

Can you imagine being invited to a political party?
It won't be much fun,
And you sure can't be naughty.
You'll be told what to say,
And handed your script.
You can think for yourself,
But must pay by the lip.
You will adhere to the cause,
Like shit to a blanket,
Remain loyal and devoted,
Then dig in at the banquet.
When you've had quite enough,
You'll be asked to step down,
Relieved of your duties,
Like a failed party clown.

Here's Joey

Sleepy Joggy Joe, he's asleep or he's out joggin'
Does he know what's going on?
Not right now! He's clearly noddin'.

Now Sea Here

What the hell is wrong with you?
Why don't people listen?
There's so much more to life than gold!
It doesn't have to glisten.
The more you have,
The more you want,
Your dough has proved and risen;
It's helped to build you brick by brick,
And now you have your prison.
A window with a coastal view,
It's nice to see the sea.
I hear that's where the fishes live,
Their net gain is they're free.

Letters to the BBC

The BBC, The BBC
C B B C, C B B
B C B C, C B C B
C B B C B C C... see?

The Tall-Tale Heart

All I've ever wanted
Is a heartfelt steady beat,
Untroubled by restrictions,
Solid ground beneath my feet.
The sound of people's laughter
At some things I've said in jest,
A day or two to treasure
When I almost did my best.
A chance to live the light fantastic,
And keep my pilot burning bright,
To hear the sound of nature's voices
And dance the rhythm of the night.
To match some goals with true successes,
And know that good is by my side,
To do just what it is I'm supposed to,
And know at least I always tried.

BBC Crisis, Crisis

We're in crisis here at the BBC
Cause our footy man went AWOL.
But he's back and doing
What he does best —
Making a big hole in our payroll.

Races Run

I've laughed and cried,
I've loved and lost,
I've learned my lessons
And paid the cost.
I've searched and found,
I've looked and seen,
Absorbed the views
And cleared the screen.
I've heard the sounds,
And listened too,
I've waited here
And prayed for you.
I try my best,
I always do,
To keep on going
And battle through.
I've looked behind,
And seen the past,
Then looked ahead
To peace at last.
It waits for all,
Exhausted souls,
A finish line
With no more goals.

Far From Mad

I'm as far from mad
As you can possibly be.
I stepped off that plank
And sailed way out to sea.
I'm not coming back soon,
I haven't been there yet,
My friend madness and I
Know we've already met.

B Movie

Barbie the doll has a movie!
It stars Barbie and her boyfriend, Ken.
Its theme is that men hate women,
And you guessed it,
That women hate men.
How jolly and lovely and fluffy,
Something special for kids to enjoy.
Is it tongue-in-cheek, or for real folks?
Meaning men, women, each girl and boy.

Is There Anyone There?

I am never alone,
Even on my own,
There is something else here
That surrounds me.
I can take it as read,
It is living not dead,
But to shed some more light
Is beyond me.
I need all I can get,
It is still here - and yet
It seems ever so hard to locate.
I have looked high and low,
Far and wide to and fro,
But despite that, I'm always too late.

Princess Tiny Tears

Little Princess Tiny Tears,
The girl who oft gets bullied,
Has thrown her toys out of the pram,
And is feeling rather sullied.
It got so bad from all us Brits
Who made her life so tearful,
She went back home to have a moan,
Which has made us much more cheerful.

Humanity

There are many types of human form,
The variety is endless.
All in all they find a path,
Their potential is tremendous.
Boys and girls from far and wide,
A credit to every nation,
Looking for love to learn and train
A trip from station to station.
Free to choose and free to speak,
Adventure with much to cherish.
And so it goes for them they those
Who live before they perish.

Poet Tree

I'm a poet but don't know it.
Plant a thought, then just grow it.
Make each line, bump and rhyme,
And it works every time.
When you think, let it sync,
And before you can blink,
There'll be more at your door,
So open up, to be sure.

Damnation

In the land of the damned, if you do
You'll be damned, whatever you do.
So… either or neither or whether or neither,
Makes no difference to them or to who.
They wait for mistakes to be made,
And sit back in the land of afraid,
Full of promise and poise,
Built on bluster and noise,
That's the snigger and sneery brigade.

Remember, Remember

Your version of events
Is a personal one,
It's the light in your eyes
You reflect on.
Formed from magical tricks,
And a gathering of sticks,
That ignite your own firework crescendo.

Fairy Dust

Little things exist, you know?
They fill the space where air is.
It helps explain why some folks see
Thems end of garden fairies.

Expect Experts, and Light Drivel

I'm an expert in my chosen field.
Perfection, precision, optimum yield.
I can see where you're all going terribly wrong -
You're all very weak, whereas I'm very strong.
I can help you to put all your failings right
By talking nonsense, and making up shite.
It's really quite easy, you should all have a go,
Just shake your head gently, and keep saying no,
Then quote some statistics —
There's plenty about —
All checked out by experts
With kudos and clout.
So that's all agreed then,
We'll leave it to them,
They know what they're doing -
Where, why, what and when.

Double Ducks

I'd like to be a little duck
What flies around being quackers.
My cause would be assisted by
The fact I'm nuts and crackers.

Dead Poetic

I wouldn't say I'm a social guy.
I do my best and I sure do try!
I'm usually wrong, but sometimes right.
I talk some sense, but mostly shite.
So, worry not if you've been offended,
My mouth and arse are open-ended.
My heart will often rule my head,
But without my heart, then I'd be dead.
With open mind and shackles loose,
I craft myself a sturdy noose.
The trap door never lets me down,
It stays in place to save the clown.
So, all I say is meant to be —
There will be no apology.

Wishful Thinking

I hope my dreams and wishes
Will eventually come true.
And one wish that I have
Is for yours to come true, too.

Match of the Days

My days are very similar,
In fact they're all the same.
They kick off every morning
Like a rescheduled football game.
They dribble up to lunchtime
For a breather and a snack,
Then continue after half-time,
And go all out on attack.
As we approach the final whistle
I look forward to my tea,
And pray I'll get the winner
From a shoot-out penalty.
The after-game cool down
Is a glass or two of wine,
And the day is finally ended
With me horizontal and supine.

Little Gems

Little people gems, little people gems,
Get them while they're small.
Little people gems, little people gems,
God bless us, short and tall.

A Poem

Here's the poem for this week's blog.
It's lots of words, some rhyming,
Like bells on strings,
With pings and tings.
It leads to all things chiming,
A symphony of A's and B's,
And many more resounding.
It keeps it neat, an upbeat treat,
With more words like astoun-ding!

One Man Banned

I have to wash and cook and clean,
I even use the hoover.
The cat attacks me when I do,
So it's best that I remove her.
I avoid her when she's in a mood
In case she might have rabies.
It seems we men can do it all,
Except, of course, have babies.

Huw Must Be Nuts?

I'm a BBC presenter,.
I present myself to kids.
Agewise, on the borderline,
But still just teapot lids.
It's best if they are troubled,
Doing gear,
In need of bunce.
That's when my help is needed,
News-reading star, and part-time nonce.

Here is the News... from the BBC

The BBC, The BBC,
Ha, ha , ha; hee, hee, hee.
The BBC, The BBC,
Ho, ho, ho; tee, hee, hee.
The BBC, The BBC,
You pay for all this,
It doesn't come free.

Not To Be Sniffed At

Our canine friends are very wise,
They can smell a rat a mile off.
They're being employed to sniff your health,
And can tell if you have kill cough.
They find other things you may not know
Are lurking in your system.
Especially at the airports,
When the scanners sometimes miss them.
So if you go to get a test
Where doggy sniffs your doodah,
Make sure you're clean and not just washed,
Or there'll be a right old hoohah.

Baa Baa Black Hole (A Sheepish Tale)

Baa baa black sheep,
Have you any wool?
Yes sir, yes sir
Three bags full.
One for the master, one for the dame,
And one for the little boy who's knitting a big black hole.

The Theory Theory

I have a little theory,
And it goes some think like this:
A theory-less society
Would be nothing more than bliss.
It would sit within its kingdom,
Doing this that and the other,
Comparing time and space and matter
With instructions from big brother.
It could think outside the bubble,
But only with permission,
Sent away to get re-training
For the ultimate transition.
Once re-educated,
And programmed to receive,
It can check out any time it likes,
But it can never ever leave.

Looking Good

Look once, look twice, look thrice…
… Looks nice.

Super Cat Curio

There is a cat who lives
A few doors down along my street.
He purrs and meows as all cats do,
But oddly has six feet.
Stranger still, I have to say,
Belief it simply begs,
I noticed just the other day,
He only has three legs.

Twat Talk

So, well, look,
I can't speak to that.
But, yeah, no, I know…
I talk like a twat.

You Lookin' At Me?!

You look at your phone,
You look at your phone,
You look at your phone again.
You look at your phone,
You look at your phone,
You look at your phone and then...
…you look at your phone... again.

Train of Thought

The train is speeding up now
As it heads on down the tracks.
It has more fuel than needed,
But there's something that it lacks.
The driver's cab is empty,
The brake is unengaged,
People stare out the windows
Watching players on the stage.
It's heading for the buffers,
Somewhere up ahead.
Time is running out now,
Has every word been said?
So build more track directions,
Go stand up on the plate,
And pull up on that handle
Before it's all too late.

Millions to One

There are a million and one things
You're expected to do,
Then a million and one more after that.
There is no end in sight,
So keep up the good fight,
Just be grateful you're here where it's at.

Piddly Poo Pants (The piddly poopy puppy)

I bought a puppy the other day,
I've called him piddly poo pants.
Cause all he ever seems to do
Is piddle pee and poo pants.
It's not that he's a naughty dog,
He's very cute and cuddly,
But every time he has a drink
He leaves a great big puddly.
It's very hard to tell him off,
He always looks so happy,
But if this piddling doesn't stop
He's going in a nappy.
It's not just all the piddle though
That makes life really tricky,
He poops as well, three times a day,
And sometimes he gets sicky.
It's no surprise he does all this,
He eats for bloomin' Britain.
I knew I'd made a big mistake,
I should have got a kitten.

Self-Responsibility

What the hell am I doing?
The government is to blame,
They haven't told me to get changed yet,
Or even to stay dressed the same,
No info regarding breathing.
Or what I'm allowed to eat,
No tips for the colour of socks either
That I'm supposed to wear on my feet.
Do I shower as often as usual?
Am I permitted to still clean my teeth?
Can I put the TV on with the toaster?
Do I wear boxers or switch into briefs?
When I walk, do I start with my right foot?
If I nap, is it for more than an hour?
Can I sit in the garden on Tuesdays?
If I water my plants, will they flower?
I can't cope with the Tories, they're rubbish,
They should be helping me minute by minute.
What do I do if my nose runs?
Catch up with it, blow it and bin it?

Now and Then

They're infecting all the rain clouds
And poisoning the water.
Your child is growing up now,
Your son is now your daughter.
The past is now the present,
The future is here to see,
I'd love to travel backwards
To nineteen sixty-three.
A childhood safe and happy,
With summers long and hot,
And winters cold and brutal
Saved by my Mum's hotpot.
No morning daily news rows
Or fake tales on your phone,
A time when all that mattered
Was getting home sweet home.
A teatime treat on telly,
The hilarious Sooty and Sweep,
With humour and violence aplenty,
When flour and water were cheap.

The Baftas

Some talent amongst
A cauldron of tripe.
The odd little sparkler,
But mostly luvvies and hype.

Swim Meat

A length or two
For you to do,
A gala meet to swim in.
It doesn't matter who you are,
As long as you aren't women.

Reliable Sources

Tomato, HP, Lea and Perrins,
Tabasco, Mayonnaise, Piri-Piri.

Mind How You Go

Re-combobulate your mind,
Learn slowly to think much faster.
Time to go and find yourself.
You are the slave and your own master.

Of Mice and Men

I hope you managed to escape, little mouse,
Through the gaps in the walls
And out of the house,
Then back to the place
Where she'd taken you from,
To your cosy warm nest,
Your own home sweet home.
It isn't her fault,
She's a cat, don't you see?
She was making a gift
Of yourself just for me.
I've told her before
Not to do such a thing,
Even love has its way
To deliver a sting.
So, I pray you'll forgive her
And watch how you go,
I'll remind her each day now,
Little mice gifts are, NO!

Mansions Sanctions

Sanctions on mansions,
And dodgy transactions
For the fat cats and oligarch wealthy.
With a big boat here
And a huge house there
Plus balances on the high side of healthy.
Fingers in pies,
A labyrinth of lies,
Reporting direct to the Kremlin.
For the tinkers and tailors
And soldiers and spies,
In the works is a well sanctioned gremlin.

Two oh Eight

I woke at two oh eight.
I'd been waiting by the gate.
She's never ever late.
I woke at two oh eight.

He-Men

Here at castle grey skull,
My brain is getting number.
I suppose it's probably all because
I'm getting dumb and dumber.
I get told off for thinking,
So I keep it lower level,
Beware of all those words you use,
You're in league with him — the Devil.
So what about all the he-men?
Have they reached their final hour?
Or is it just a change of slogan,
I used to have the power.

Dug Up

I'm trying to dig myself out of a hole.
The harder I dig,
The deeper I go.
So maybe I won't dig myself anymore,
I'll just stay right here
On the lower ground floor.

You're Kraken Me Up

Release the Kraken,
So the saying goes,
A mythical deadly creature
Designed to mess with what's left of your health.
With many a cunning feature,
Try vitamins D and C, my friends.
In a bid to remain mostly healthy,
A much better place to reside and enjoy
Than the land of the sick and the wealthy.

Like Clockwork

Some poems would be nice, I think to myself,
And the wheels and the cogs start churning.
They whir and they click,
Like a tock needs to tick,
And the rhyming and chiming keep turning.
They riddle me this,
Then they riddle me that,
To question the point and the meaning.
But the opening act
Is a matter of fact —
I'm allowed a discreet private screening.

As It Beats Within

People are wary of poets,
I have no idea why that should be.
We're connected to words by a rhythm,
A wavelength that no one can see.
But the heart plays a drum we can all hear,
Whether sleeping or wide-eyed awake,
And that music just never stops playing,
Time and motion do not take a break.

Exposed

Expose yourself to life's harsh realities —
What doesn't kill you makes you stronger.
Stand up and be counted,
Be just who you are,
And there's a chance of you living much longer.

Every Spring is Everything

After winter must come spring.
Green shoots appear and with them bring
Blossoms determined to rise and shine.
All will emerge as matter of time.

The Laboured Party

Was we your choice?
I sure hope we was.
We is rough and tough and dead good.
We is a rudderless ship,
And our leader's a drip,
Just a big pile of rotten dead wood.

The BBC

The BBC and their dear licence fee
Take your money and claim to be neutral,
But they sway to the left,
They're not subtle or deft,
And their treatment of Tories is brutal.
It is high time they went
With their twisted and bent
Or just focus on making good telly.
But tune into the news,
And the one-sided views,
Will confirm that it's 'not on your nelly'.

Here Today...

There's a ghost at my side
And it carries a scythe,
And from time to time it reminds me,
That the deep final cut
Is most certain yet but —
No point hiding —it is going to find me.

You Must be Joking

Tell me something funny, please,
I love a laugh and titter.
I'm sick of all these snowflake types,
Offended, weak and bitter.
You can't say this,
You can't say that,
How dare you very dare you!
Well, stay at home you weary creep,
Enjoy your own woke curfew.

Global List

Upon this tiny spinning globe,
A spec in time and space,
The starter fired the starting gun
To start the human race.
For many years we lagged behind,
Our progress far too slow,
But then we caught up with the pack,
With everything we know.
We galloped on, our knowledge won,
On toil and serious thought.
And yet it seems it may have been
Endeavours all for nought.

Plucking Numbers

Numbers plucked from thin fresh air
That change like stormy weather.
Stop pulling on that cord, you see
It's my worn-out end of tether.

Small Talk

It's the little things in life
That are most overlooked.
So, get rid of those uncalled for sweeties.
They may be quite small,
Shrunken gum drops, that's all
Don't those woke folk get right on your titties.

Arty Fishy Oil in Telly Gents

AI will take care of our stories now,
And invent them as if they were yours.
They'll even branch out into poetry,
But there's probably a good chance you'll be able to spot
them a mile off I would imagine...
Some will be better than others,
Some will be poorer than some,
Some will be gushingly awful,
And some will be comfortably dumb.
So, what shall we write now we're done for,
Replaced by circuits and maths with no soul?
Let's head out to space with our memories,
And disappear down a swirling black hole.

New World Order

I don't know how the world works.
It appears to have its own mind,
Spinning hot rock to begin with,
Then manifestations of every kind,
Water and plants and creatures
In a race to the top of the tree.
Somewhere in time we were monkeys,
But right now we are just you and me.

Is Non-Rhymin' Crimin' or just Void of Timin'?

Sometimes,
Not always
But certainly,
Mostly,
With rhyming
There's more
To adore...
Without it,
It's timeless
And rhymeless
And spineless.
On your way out
Do please close the door.

Away with Words!

There is a way with words, they say,
Whether written, heard, or spoken.
But words are words,
Just let them be,
Politely left unwoken.

And the Winner... is?

And the winner is... no body.

Eat, Drink, and be Wary

It's Christmas Day, hip hip hooray!
I've got some food and drink in,
I've peeled the spuds and steamed the pud,
Now time to squeeze a snooze in.
Oh, lordy no! Me bird is burned,
And all me veg cremated!
I had to drink a bit too much
And end up totes sedated.
But fear ye not, for mighty dread
Had spared me pigs in bacon.
The smell of smokey, porky treats
Had caused me to awaken.
So all's not lost, I shall not starve,
I've saved some Christmas dinner.
It's just a bit more healthier,
So everyone's a winner.

Fully Booked

You said you were coming
But you never showed up.
There were other folks waiting
But we stood them up.
Just do me a favour,
Don't act like a jerk,
If you let us know something
Then everything works.

Twas the Night Before

Twas the night before Crimbo,
My vision somewhat blurred,
As with tin of soup in hand
I hurried homewards undeterred.
I avoided carol singers
And their merry Christmas songs,
Then picked a piece of coal or two
To place on fire with fireside tongs.
Once wrapped in warming blanket,
I began my evening feast,
Then was rudely interrupted
By some fiendish ghostly beast.
It was me, but much, much older,
Come to tell me of my fate,
Should I fail to realise it
Before it all becomes too late.
I ignored the foolish spectre
And made ready for my bed,
Drifting off into a slumber,
Forgetting all the spook had said.
It was not a dreamless rest, though,
I awoke at one two three,
Then again at half-past seven
As I was bursting for a pee.
It had all just been a nightmare,
Fuelled by scoops of strongish ales.
Oh! I do love Christmas spirits
And their drunken Christmas tales.

Christmas Fair

The church hall was decked with Christmas,
The stage arranged with all things stable.
There was mistletoe and holly,
And gifts and food laid on a table.
The tree was twinkling in its glory
As attendee numbers swelled,
They had come to hear the story,
The greatest story ever telled!
But due to current legislation,
Masks and distance rulings too,
The hall was not allowed the many
But instead a lowly few.
As the play approached, the ending,
Where a doll is always dropped,
Someone pushed the hall door open
And a champagne bottle popped.
'It's Christmas everybody!'
Spoke an angel with no mask,
'Give us half a chance to party,
Is that way too much to ask?'
She was tasered, cuffed and mace-sprayed
As the shepherds watched in horror,
Then the whole event was cancelled
Until Tier Two which starts tomorrow.

The Little Baby Cheeses

The little baby Jesus
Comes but once in every year,
To raise our flagging spirits
And top our tummies up with beer.
He looks after all the children,
Their faces rosy and aglow,
That's from wearing masks though,
Not from Santa's ho ho ho!
He fills their sacks with presents,
Sprinkles Santa with some dust,
That allows him to fly faster
With the reindeer that he trusts.
To every corner of the planet,
For boys and girls both good and bad,
With a message and not just presents,
To fill our hearts and make us glad.
Once the gifts have all been opened
And the rubbish cleared away,
It's nice to sit and think what matters
When that day is Christmas day.

Miss Information

She's as sly as a fox
And twice as cute,
Don't believe all she says,
She's just here for the shoot.
Telling tales she will whisper
Whether you listen or look,
For your eyes and your ears
She has baited the hook.
Wake up intuition,
Let it proof-read the text,
If you don't and it's loaded
It will target you next.

Proper Gander

Take a look,
A real good look
At what you need to see.
Don't avert your gaze
In the swirling haze,
Oh, look! There's he and she.

Savile Row

The smartest of suits,
All entirely self-made,
Stitched up by the best,
Checked out by the rest,
Cloth accordingly cut,
In both texture and depth.
Never mind, 'how's the quality?',
Just make sure there's some width.

The Conservative Party

Here at the Conservative Party
We are honest and true to our word.
You are angry, and some may well doubt this,
With some stuff you have recently heard.
But just look at our splendid track record,
And the roll out of things that don't work,
We never don't not have no parties,
Said a spokesman with more than a smirk.

Two-Four-Six

I woke at two four six,
My mind a swirling mix
Of treats, but mostly tricks.
I woke at two four six,

All will be Revealed

Can you see it yet?
Can you feel the beat?
Can you hear the roar approaching?
Are you standing tall?
Are you holding firm?
Are you tired of all the coaching?
Do you feel the heat?
Do you hear the call?
Do you see the bright blue yonder?
For the corn is tall
And the scythes are sharp,
And there's much for all to ponder.

Bi-cycle

I've entered a race
I shouldn't be in,
But I so bloomin' well want to win it.
I know I'm a man,
But I'm so very tran,
So it should be allowed —
Yeah? No?... innit?

Reasons to Continue Being Silly... 10, 11, 12

Grand old Duke of York,
Slice of belly pork,
Use your knife and fork.
Gin and slimline tonic,
Simply supersonic,
Heartburn getting chronic.
Loss of understanding,
Light switch on the landing,
Re-adjust your branding.
Milk and cookie treat,
Keep it nice and neat,
Ground beneath your feet.
Soon be time for tennis,
Flies a blinkin' menace,
So is that lad Dennis.
Parlez vous Francais?
Wacky doodah day,
Always have your say.
Try and keep it simple,
Oh, my God, a pimple!
No, it's just a dimple.
Lack of bloomin' wealth,
Park it on the shelf,
Think about your health.
Reasons to continue being silly... ten, eleven, twelve.

Very Superstitious

'Listen here,' said the deaf man,
Who could see the way ahead,
'Better instinct and intuition
Than be hopelessly misled.'
Think to look before you leap peeps
Caution always smells a rat.
Take a step back and choose wisely
The most inviting welcome mat.
Never overstay your visit,
Leave some room upon the hill,
Trouble no one with your business,
Pay for all goods at the till.

Right This Way

Write off, right on,
Tune in, time out,
Get down, jump up,
So sure, no doubt.
Try this, use that,
Say less, hear more,
In here, leave there,
Front gate, back door.

Move On Up

Back and forth, to and fro,
Side to side, quick and slow.
Up and down, inside out,
Up the pole, down the spout.
To the left, to the right,
Up on top, out of sight.
Far away, in your face,
Out of town, stay in place.
Move on up, don't back down,
Sensible, silly clown.
Overrule, underfoot,
Strike for more, take a cut.
Sit and think, dream away,
Leave for good, cause to stay.
Wave goodbye, blow a kiss,
Life is life, hit and miss.

Elected

Orange Don, or Creepy Joe,
Post your vote, let us know.
Don't you worry, no need to hurry,
Take it steady, whenever you're ready.
What are the scores on the doors?
Err... Forfar five, East Fife four.
Quite remarkable.

Free Spirit (buy one, get one free)

Sometimes, when you're in a tunnel,
The dark becomes your friend.
It sits and listens to your words,
Aware of where you end.
The tunnel has two openings,
One each at either side,
The choice is yours, which way you go,
There is no place to hide.
Until your work is done, my friend,
The tunnel holds the key,
And tilts towards the end that helps
To set your spirit free.

One in Ten

Don't go getting eager,
There could be worse to come.
This all-embracing fever,
Preventing all our fun.
But here comes Johnny Vaccine,
A nine of ten success.
I hope I'm nine in line then,
Not blinkin' number ten.

Like Clockwork

Don't things really wind you up,
This or they and them or that?
An eye for an eye, a tooth for a tooth,
The simple truth or tit for tat.
Some you win and some you lose,
Calm and collect or blow a fuse.
Reap what you sow, build a bridge,
Go without food, seek privilege.
Times pass by, pigs do fly,
Me oh me, my oh my.
Make some sense, score some points,
Swollen toes, aching joints.
Stay at home, out and about,
Meek and mild, loads of clout.
Stand up straight, sit down there,
Shoulders back, grin and bear.
Ready steady, run your race,
Keep the faith, don't lose face.
All in all, have a ball,
Room to grow, ten feet tall.
Seek him here, seek him there,
Open up, hide your fear.
Go on a roll, shut up shop,
Set your sights, come out on top.

Missed Err President

Old Trumpster, he's a boy alright!
He talks some tripe and tweets some shite,
But on the whole, he's just a chap.
The odd faux pas, the odd mishap.
His fans can't get enough of him,
The swamp dogs think he's really dim.
I guess he's somewhere in between,
An orange sun and old has-been.
He's lagging badly in the polls,
His Twitter feed alive with trolls.
But Donald knows a trick or two,
Despite him having Covid flu.
Don't write him off until it's done,
Besides, the guy is so much fun.
The alternative is sleepy Joe —
Is he just tired, or is he slow?
He told the Prez to shut his trap,
Then had his turn at talking crap.
So there you have it, there it is,
A big old hit, or doggone miss.

Mission Aborted

Be to be, or not to…
Is that the question?

It's Alright for Sum

Addition and subtraction,
Multiplication and divide,
Make sure your numbers balance
Equal measures on both sides.
Pace your feet in yards and inches,
Give your head two metres space,
Read the data if you need to,
Slip away without a trace.
Tot up all the shapes and angles,
Feed the stats into a chart,
Sit back and do the maths folks,
As it tears us all apart.
If you need a pen and paper,
Show your workings as you go,
Cover up when someone's watching,
The more informed the less they know.
When you finally see the answer,
It may take you by surprise,
You have searched for many years
And it was right before your eyes.

Made in China

We welcome all with all our arms,
To our land of open prison.
The great red wall is now a wave,
Restricted sound and vision.

Folk Law

We should all make up some stories
About our future present past,
And let history sit in judgment,
Should they fade or should they last?
Always start at the beginning,
Followed by a middle and an end,
Then some bits to fill the spaces
On which the outcome will depend.
The characters in the mixture
Will assist the ebb and flow,
Then as it grows its branches,
The roots will go where they will go.
And then you've grown a family tree,
A root and branch endeavour,
It stands amongst a forest
Where the folklore lasts forever.

Window Pain

The shapes and sizes passing by
Make you wonder what they're thinking.
They peer inside with googly eyes
With some not even blinking.
Some come on in, some head on out,
Their fashions tell a story.
An eclectic mix of Britain's best —
A land of hope and glory.

The Pinocchio Theory

Constructed from timber,
A childhood of wood,
Unable to do things
Those other kids could.
A puppet in real terms,
With fine strings and joints,
A nose that grows outwards
To form a long point.
A kindly creator,
Who wished on a star,
No matter what, when, where,
Whoever you are.
Your dreams are your future,
So keep them in mind,
Try not to be wooden,
Be gentle and kind.

Little Miss Muffet

Little Miss Muffet,
Sat on her tuffet,
Eating her curds and whey.
Along came a spider
And sat down beside her —
Unbelievable!
Not a moment's peace and bloody quiet anywhere.

Bigot Tree

I have the same sized tree
As you, my friend.
I acquired it at birth.
It came to me, delivered for free,
From my dear friend, Planet Earth.
The club I was assigned to
Was the, 'You're free to make your choice'.
You can sit there and do nothing,
Or you can learn and find your voice.
Sometimes, no one listens,
Occasionally, they're all ears,
Frightened to keep on talking,
Paralysed with fears
That their words won't meet approval
From some members of the club.
Ah yes, I remember them, those that
Have their own little country hub.

Happy Peeps

Happy people, happy minds,
Funny people, funny minds,
Nosey people, nosey minds,
Private people... Venetian blinds.

Pure Hogwashery

It's time to give your hogs a wash,
They're piggin' filthy dirty.
You want them spick and span and clean,
Especially if you're flirty.
No one likes a stinky swine
Who reeks from head to toe,
Report all mingin' pork to me,
Our survey needs to know.

Pregnant Pause

There's a new thing for the ladies,
It's called the menopause.
It's only just been noticed,
Despite being around for many years.
There are over forty symptoms,
Some of which you'll never know.
It makes you wonder how they managed,
All those thousands of years ago.

Stopwatch

Does anyone have the right time?
'There is no such thing,' said the clock.
'Nobody knows when it started.
So, keep watching, you'll know when to stop.'

Midsummer Murder

Midsummer weather is murder, you know.
Although it's nice and warm and sunny,
But the water's all gone,
And me house is on fire,
So why do I find all that funny?

Half Measures

Let's halve inflation and waiting lists too,
Let's do everything by halves if we can,
Let's halve the entire population,
And drink halves direct from the can.
Let's halve all our troubles and worries,
Let's go halves on paying the bill,
Let half of the nation eat healthy,
And let half take the bitterest pill.
Watch half of your glass looking empty,
While the other half looks like half full,
Expect half of the day to be sunny,
And the other half gloomy and dull.
Take half an hour break at lunchtime,
Eat half of the butty you bought,
Then go home and work out your expenses,
Minus two halves that leaves you with nought.

Reasons to be Poorly - Part 3

Wake up feeling groggy,
Head a little foggy,
Go and walk the doggy.
Check the heart is pumping,
Not much time for humping,
Bathroom for a dumpling.
Grab your pills and swallow,
Empty, feeling hollow,
Fry up soon to follow!
Have a look at fit-bit,
Spy a tasty tit-bit,
God, you are a nit-wit.
Now you feel all weary,
Could be all the beery,
This isn't working... clearly.
Reasons to be poorly – 1, 2, 3.
(Why don't you get back into bed?)

Clock... Watch

Tik tok, tik tok.
Whats app?... Nothing.

Reasons to be Fearful - Part 3

Fake tan in a bottle,
Orange skin with mottle,
Give yer kid a throttle.
Half a pound of innit,
Blow yer nose and bin it,
Never seen or sin it.
Take a pill to cure it,
Get some more and score it,
Get in gear and floor it.
Have two slugs for eyebrows,
Stay at home and have rows,
Fill the role of cash cows.
Wave two fingers lairy,
Think that you're a fairy,
Limit cheese and dairy.
Chicken in a bucket,
Twenty pieces, cluck it,
Maybe learn to cook it.
Reasons to be fearful – 1, 2, 3.

Hey, Good Looking

She ain't bad looking,
She's got a great look!
That's bound to be helpful
When she needs a good... appropriate partner to settle down with.

Pin the Tale on the Elephant in the Room... (What... a Donkey?)

Trumpster's in trouble again.
So I see.
For the trumpteenth time this year.
Can't you find a squeaky-clean candidate?
Good luck with that one... I'll wait here.

Coronation Chicken

I like a good curry,
Whatever the season,
Be it summer or winter or spring.
Yet I can't help but wonder,
If I'm making a blunder,
Having chapati to see in the King.

Train of Thought

Unopposed and undisclosed,
Thoughts queue to form a line
That stretches back
And fades to black,
A distant light in time.

Bitter Twitter (All Elon the Watchtower)

Twitter's a site
Where you can say what you want,
Just as long as the censors agree.
They have their opinions,
Controlled as they are,
But that doesn't include you and me.
So, it has a new owner
Who is doing quite well,
He is wealthy and bolshie and brusque.
You can have your voice back,
Now they're cutting some slack,
Thanks to spaceman.
Blast off! Elon Musk.

Sweet Dreams

I'll try again tomorrow,
If I get another chance,
To listen to the music
And lead a merry dance.
I'll help to lift some spirits,
And hope they find their way.
Our time is very precious,
And today could be the day.

Timely

A poem I have not written
In these last six days plus one.
It was Friday, then was Thursday,
Where has all that time now gone?
It's still here and always watching,
An eye on what the present passed,
The guardian of all that happens,
Time for all the questions asked.

May Bee

What may be May bee, maybe.
What you say, what you think,
What you do or don't see,
But maybe, just maybe,
You'll be as you'll be,
Or maybe, just May bee,
You will maybe leave be.

Royal Protection

Harry makes his Granny laugh,
He makes me chuckle too.
He's here to make sure she is safe,
A full-on loyal, royal blue.

Big Bother

Big Bother knows your details,
It tracks you everywhere.
It watches while you're driving,
To see how far you dare.
It listens to your phone calls,
And programs your TV.
It recognises features,
And you reckon that you're free?
It knows how much you're earning,
And every time you spend,
You think it's all just started —
Wait and see where all this ends.
It wants all that you have, friend,
It wants your very soul,
It doesn't just want pieces,
It wants to eat you whole.

Two Three Eight

I woke at two three eight,
Concerned about my fate.
I'm here, so not too late.
I woke at two three eight.

High Vis Racket

Have you seen my yellow jacket, mate?
It means that I'm in charge.
And what concerns me mostly
Is that you're clearly out at large.
What's your name and where you going?
You should be home being mentally ill.
So, do everything I tell you,
Forget you ever had free will.
Look into my eyes and tell me
That you never bend the rules.
You're a problem that needs solving,
Just like the other healthy fools.

Looking Up

It's easy to make blind assumptions.
Well, it is if your vision is blurred.
A similar thing tends to happen
When you're drunk and your language is slurred.
So, err on the side of caution,
Regard all the facts as they grow,
Then try hard not to raise expectations,
Keep them ticking on middle to low.
It's then you may find some contentment,
In the nooks and the crannies of days,
And by chance, if you're ever so lucky,
You'll discover a mending of ways.

Jibberwacky (no relation to *Jabberwocky*)

The Jibberwacky lived at a fork in the road,
In a cabin he'd built with his savings.
It was cosy and warm and full of good charm,
Save a cupboard crammed full of his shavings.
These clippings of hair brought some magic to bear,
As when held to the light with a spy glass,
You could see lots of things, like cogs and springs,
That told tales of a new road and by-pass.
They appeared in a way only he knew to say,
So, in theory a built-in defence code.
When others did try to give them the eye,
They lay still and unseen in stealth mode.
They told of a time that ran backwards in-line
To a place you could hope, pray and dream for,
Full of happy and funny with no need for money,
And a porthole instead of a door.

Pick and Pox

Pick a pox, any pox,
The choice is up to you.
Get a bracelet that says,
'You're ill all the time'.
Now there's something catchy and new!

Brass in Pocket

I need to earn a living wage.
How can I cope on fifty-nine grand?
There are some folk who get
Much more money than me,
When can I join that big-bucks brass band?

Herd Impunity

The herd in itself is a dangerous beast,
Made of multiple creatures
Who are keen for the feast.
But the one who moves first
Is quite a different breed.
Not a kick will it get
When the cattle stampede.

Women's Own

What is a woman,
I hear you ask,
Such a difficult thing to determine.
Is it a lake or a stream,
Or is it all just a dream?
And just who is it really concerning?

About Time

In a minute or two,
With those seconds that flew,
And the hours then turn into days.
It all happens so fast,
Present, future and past,
We are passing our time through the haze.

Who's Up for the Cup?

Boris has finally run out of track,
As the stabbers form orderly queues at his back,
Then tell us how honest and faithful they are,
Whilst drinking and groping their friends at the bar.
But the race is now on to see who fancies a crack
At the chalice of poisoned political crap.

Planet Rwanda

There's a flight on the runway,
And it's ready to go,
All it needs is a boat load of migrants.
But it seems they would rather
Stay in the good old UK
Than in the EU or a hot-bed for tyrants.

We're All Going On A…

We are all of us going,
But just when, where and how?
It's a problem for solving,
Though perhaps not right now.
Take steps on your journey,
And never ask why,
Just head where you're going,
But don't try and fly.

You See The Problem?

You're damned if you do,
And you're damned if you don't,
So don't damned do nothing,
And damned do you won't.

Leader of the Peck

Like a pack of hungry wolves
Closing in towards its prey,
Pecking order is important,
Farmyard antics, come what may.

Three Strikes and You're Out

All for one, and three for all,
We must unite and stand together.
Let's go on strike,
Let's do no work,
And enjoy the sunny weather.

How it Works

There are many splendid things
That our little planet brings,
Based on science and wonder and nature.
But they are all of man's doing,
Whether completed or in ruin,
Depending on complicated legislature.

Vote Confidently

Tick a box of your choice,
To enable your voice,
In selecting the view you prefer.
Then sit back and enjoy,
Watching ploy after ploy,
As your dreams are replaced by defer.

Where Next?

Where next, I hear you asking?
As we tread the narrow way,
A fight to speak with freedom,
A chance for all to have their say,
A check on all you're thinking
On just exactly where you stand —
Or kneel or sit or lie down,
Then rise again behind your brand.
Which direction is it taking,
The cause you follow with your heart?
It is written in your fabric,
And has been there from the start.

Living Costs

There is a price you pay to live on Earth,
And those costs they are a-rising.
For knowledge, all you pay is attention.
Now isn't that surprising?

Hooked

I try hard to forget what it meant to me,
I try hard to forget how it looked.
But like a fish in the river of life, it seems,
There's a chance you just simply get hooked.

No One's Safe!

No one's safe until everyone's safe,
Preached the slogan man down to the many.
But no one is sure, said a man to the wise,
Not one single man, woman, not any.
For to always be safe,
Means do nothing, then die,
And all in between would be wasted.
So much better to live,
And risk all that you give,
On a life that has truly been tasted.

Time Trial

There's no point trying to look for it,
It's right before your eyes.
As honest as the day is long,
The truth is that time flies.
A waiting game with time to spare,
Too late to stop it starting,
A lifespan split down into ticks,
For all on time departing.
A gauge to keep you all on track,
In search of pain or pleasure,
A ticking timebomb, well aware
That simply has your measure.

One-Off Original

It's hard to be original
If you're not the first one here.
Everything keeps repeating,
It happens year on year.
You're a collection of occurrences,
A multitude of fears,
A gathering of incidents,
Of dreams and joy and tears.
We are the fruit of Earth and daylight,
A life of pleasure and pain.
We are but flowers in the garden,
Enjoy the sunshine and the rain.

Your Clarity Has Transpired

I've clarified my clarity,
It's now transparent as transparent can be.
Why don't you just use normal words,
Like truth and honesty?

Word Salad

Never be afraid to articulate
With the words that YOU want to use.
And if they tell you that they know better,
Tell them you feel bullied, oppressed and abused.

Happy New Tier Everyone

Toodle pip to twenty-twenty,
Well hello there twenty-one.
Bye-ze-bye the Euro Union,
Welcome to our new free-dom.
Au revoir to fishy dealings,
Look ahead and make net gains,
Worry not regarding travel,
Be it boat or planes or trains.
Keep an eye out for the virus,
It's a sneaky little shit,
Is it fearful of the vaccine — are you kidding?
Not one bit?
It just puts a new disguise on,
A false moustache and silly hat,
I bet you're scared now, aren't you?
Good, job done, then that is that.
No, I jest of course, don't worry,
All will be well in the end,
Check your pulse and then your signal,
Log your data then hit send.
When your info has been processed,
We'll assess your total worth,
And make a judgement on your future,
Here on Tier 5 Planet Earth.

This Train

There's a train that's always running,
And it picks up as it goes,
It stops at every station,
You'll have seen it, I suppose?
It wears a coat of many colours
So it's impossible to miss,
It travels with tranquillity
To awe-inspiring bliss.
The ticket costs you nothing
Other than an open heart,
And an empty mind that welcomes
Love and kindness from the start.

Mornin' All

Good morning one, good morning all,
Good morning short, good morning tall.
Good morning stout, good morning slim,
Good morning bright, good morning dim.
Good morning less, good morning more,
Good morning rich, good morning poor.
Good morning each and every one,
God bless your day, go have some fun.

More Clarity Please

I'm running out of clarity,
I thought I'd bought enough,
I drink it by the bucket full
When times are really tough.
It isn't clear and see-through,
It's red and rather silky,
Unlike that bland transparent stuff,
All tasteless bleak and milky.
I'm not sure how much more I need,
I'm nearly at my limit,
I can't keep letting my hair down —
Perhaps I'd better trim it.

Two One One

I woke at two one one,
Unsure of where I'm from.
You're here, and then you're gone,
I woke at two one one.

Inconsequential

So many things matter,
So many things shouldn't,
So many folks chatter,
I wish that they wouldn't.

Something or Nothing

Something or nothing,
Either or neither,
Ever or never,
One or none.
Up and down,
On or off,
In and out,
Sure or doubt.
Itchy and scratchy,
Picky and choosy,
Day and night,
Dark or light.
Happy as Larry,
Single or marry,
Here and now,
When and how.
For or agin,
Lose or win,
Stay or leave,
Just believe.
Hope and pray —
Find a way!

No Doubt – II

So do I let the darkness in,
Or do I stand and fight?
A chance to reinvent myself,
And head towards the light?
Have I the time to reignite and see my spirit fly,
Or do I simply fade away and never even try?
With faith and hope on turning tide,
I rise to tell my tale,
And bless the breeze that bares no ill
That gently fills my sail.
This doubt I have is all of me,
This doubt I have is mine,
No doubt that it belongs to me
To stop my rise and shine.
A doubt I never welcomed here,
It hides where I can't see.
It lies within the soul of me,
And never lets me be.